Increase Understanding
LEARN
the art of acting

Judah Kenaz

ISBN: 978-1-4834-2541-2 (sc)
ISBN: 978-1-4834-2540-5 (e)

Lulu Publishing Services rev. date: 2/12/2015

CONTENTS

FOREWORD vii

PREFACE ix

ACTING 1

THE PLAY 3

INSIDE-OUT 5

OUTSIDE-IN 9

VOICE 11

ARTICULATION 13

MOTOR SKILLS 17

AUDITION 25

EMOTIONAL MEMORY RECALL 27

PERSONALIZATION 31

TALKING & LISTENING 33

COMMENTS 37

PLAY LIST 41

AFTERWORD 43

ACKNOWLEDGEMENTS 45

ABOUT THE AUTHOR 47

FOREWORD

My theme "Increase Understanding" is best begun in the library/cinema where reading plays and living out the roles in them is the seed of understanding. It's what draws us to the movies to watch the stories lived out before our eyes.

Experiencing unrequited love, for example, in the final scene of *Lili* opens your heart to the feeling of loving someone who doesn't return your love.

Deer Hunter takes us behind the scenes of war where the enemy loads the gun and hands it to his prisoner demanding that he play Russian roulette. I had been fully invested as I watched this film for the first time and broke down sobbing when he pulled the trigger.

It's no surprise that we get introduced in our teens to Shakespeare with *Macbeth* as we learn the excesses of ambition; and *Romeo and Juliet* and the power of love to lead to self-sacrifice.

On through the panoply of theater literature where we uncover jealousy between husband and wife in *Hedda Gabler* or male dominance in *Taming of the Shrew*. In *Who's Afraid of Virginia Woolf* we watch a married couple cross the line into blunt, frank, brutal truth. A new play *The Curious Incident of the Dog in the Night-Time* familiarizes us with the thinking of an autistic boy whose perceptions are spare, selective and touching.

I love the theater.

PREFACE

New York attracts artists and going to New York heightens your chance of keeping company with some of the greatest talents in theater no matter your discipline – acting, directing, designing – lights, sets, costumes, writing, dance or music.

To have the experience of dancing Joe Layton choreography or Donald Saddler's is to crawl inside a Rembrandt, learn by osmosis. Playing a scene with an actor whose work is on a higher plane than yours raises the level of your art. Don't miss the opportunity – New York!

Whether you are an aspiring actor or a parent who never plans to step on a stage, I hope to let you in on some of what I've learned in 20 years honing my skill in the Art of acting. This handbook will help you understand acting jargon **arc, beats, sides.**

Creating a character is so absorbing and the more guidelines you have at your disposal the better. You will never stop picking up tips as you go. Your imagination is your primary source of creation and having additional tools is extraordinary. My last acting job was in a repertory company where so many master acting classes were taught I felt like I finally knew how to approach creating a character. When my contract expired I retired my acting career and all these helpful colors were left on the palette.

To gamble in the arts is daring and not for the faint of heart. Rejection and self doubt are demons you learn to face but purpose will see you through. Talking to other actors is an enormous benefit. The community is the most familiar, humorous, glamorous. It is the best group of people I have ever been associated with. To create the world of the play with a cast of actors forms a bond that's oddly mystical.

ACTING

Learning to act is one of the most exciting disciplines you could undertake. In league with psychology, the art of acting takes you deep inside the motivation of a character, a role, to understand the thru-line of action a person follows to get things done.

Unlike the vagaries of reality, acting gives you control over events that in reality are governed by instinct. Acting allows you the gift of focus, sculpting reactions and that is empowering.

I watched a broadcast of an opera recently and the leading man did not understand, nor had he explored, the emotional content of his aria. His skill level was very high, he hit all the right notes but there was no "there" there.

The actor's tool box, building a character from: outside in and from inside out, talking, listening and remembering, emotional memory recall, these tools are invaluable in creating believable character with the emotional life to live out the plot.

THE PLAY

In my teens I spent the summers reading plays. My library had a limit of 8 books per visit. A play takes approximately two hours to read. I was whipping through the entire stack.

From the time I saw Gene Kelly *Singin' in the Rain* I knew I wanted to be an actor. The need to touch people as he touched me with that song led me straight to my calling.

During WWII my father served in the U.S. Navy. My mother took me to the movies every Wednesday night. She got a box of Chews and I got a box of Juicy Fruit out of the vending machine and we were off on another adventure while we waited anxiously for dad's return.

Most often I was exposed to movie acting. The mode of acting for the theater differs somewhat but both approaches demand immersion in a story told through characters and theater literature drew me to the library those summers.

Read the script straight through from beginning to end without interruption and digest the entire idea of the play.

You have entered the world of the play. Then you can begin to focus on the part your character plays. Are you passive, do things happen to you or are you aggressive and take action to get what you want.

I'll begin with familiar move roles to acquaint you with the basic analysis that follows reading the script straight through.

INSIDE-OUT

EXAMPLE: The character Sharon Stone plays in the movie *Casino*, Ginger McKenna.

Inside the life of a gangster's wife who lives on the edge in a world of suspicion, jealousy and lies, she lies to divert suspicion – she is going to have her hair done she says when she is meeting her former pimp to give him funds to cover a payoff to a business associate.

Tension is a constant in the life of this character; and it escalates with the precision of a calibrator. The development of the role, often referred to as the **arc**, once understood, intellectually and viscerally, can be plotted in your script. Analyze each scene the character appears in and parcel it out into **beats**.

A beat describes "an exchange" or an "action":e.g., she picks up the milk carton that's on the table. Make a **choice**: she is in a hurry, she shakes the carton and it's empty and she sighs in exasperation. The underlying emotion informs her action and it becomes clear as you read the entire play or script as the case may be.

Dialogue begins and the first interchange may uncover information about the fact that she wants a large sum of money. Her husband wants to know why she needs the money. End beat. He resists and finds reason why she needs to tell him why she needs the money. She counters. One of them will have the deciding argument and that ends that beat. And on we go through the scene blocking out the beats. Now the groundwork has been laid and you can see more clearly what you have to work with.

It's necessary to use a verb to define each beat – though the overall motivation remains, each beat adds fuel to the accomplishment of that motive. Example: to defend, to convince, to change, to delay, to

inform, uncover, unearth, denounce, disown, reject, resist, avenge…
and myriad other verbs that incite one to action. The stronger the verb
the better.

Let's look at Stanley Kowalski. In *A Streetcar Named Desire* he
represents arousal. Stella, being his mainstay, represents constancy.
It appears Stella represents constancy for Blanche as well. Blanche
symbolizes illusion, some might say, delusion. The interplay of this trio
constitutes the plot and the theme of *Streetcar*.

Stanley relies on Stella to balance the centerpiece of his existence.
But Stella is driven to sympathize with her sister, Blanche, watching
Stanley's taunting and teasing as he stirs the urge for elusive Blanche.
Poor wounded Stanley howls his primal scream STELLA. All that
he is misunderstood for hollers out in desperation to the one person
who really knows him.

Every actor interprets Stanley differently. That is what makes
seeing one man's Stanley for the purpose of comparing it to another's so
much fun. Within the confines of the play there are infinite variations
that will satisfy.

As actors we inhabit the life of a gangster's wife, the hormonal
young man in the French Quarter, or a Danish prince in Hamlet,
a member of an aristocratic Russian family on the brink of ruin in
the Cherry Orchard, the Lady of the Camillias on her deathbed, a
hunchback spinster living under strict commandments of purity in
the House of Bernarda Alba. We get to walk around inside the life of
a character and expand our own lives with the feelings and words of
others' lives.

I've often mused on the subject of reincarnation. Seems unfair that
my soul be judged on one set of circumstances – my life. I suppose it's
my calling but I've always wondered what it would be like to be in
other circumstances. If this sounds familiar, acting is for you.

OUTSIDE-IN

Now that your role has been broken down into beats, examine the needs of the character.

Create the character from the outside in: decide where this character is centered – in the head, gut or genitals.

Where exactly is the center of gravity? This will determine how your character moves, talks, perhaps even how he/she speaks.

Where does the character carry tension? Say it's in the head. This person is an intellectual. Tense your brain. Feel the tension determine your facial expression.

If the tension is between the shoulders - immediately an attitude takes you over. Your torso tightens and your chest inflates.

Now put the tension between your legs – another character emerges, perhaps, Stanley Kowalski.

This little exercise will draw a picture of the physicalization of the role you will play. Walk around the room holding onto those tensions. See how they move.

Now. Do your morning toilette as the character. Take your shower, brush your teeth, fix your breakfast as this character and do this every morning for a week, the first week of rehearsal and voila' your physicalization of this character is set.

VOICE

The rhythm and syntax of the dialogue, as written, is the first determinant of the character's voice.

Next will be your choice for the center of gravity. The voice is placed either in the throat, in the head or in the nose.

Such oddities as a lisp or a stutter are generally part of a character's description and shouldn't be pursued without the agreement of the director. Anything that disrupts the audience's ability to follow the play will be outlawed by the director, as it should be. But the voice is the instrument that carries the emotional pitch of your part.

To find your authentic voice, relax your throat and tongue in an exercise like this: Drop your head over your chest. Swing it left and right and work it out. Then shake your head vigorously, allowing your lips and cheeks to shake loose. It's helpful to think of yourself as drunk to get the maximum amount of relaxation. Now take ten deep breaths in through the nose for a count of 7. Out through the mouth for a count of 10, pursing your lips, breathing out until your diaphragm contracts.

Projection, reaching the back row with your performance, requires precise enunciation and some attention needs be paid to this skill. It needn't overtake you as an actor. Like any discipline you use the skill as you will.

Conviction will carry to the end of a sentence and it helps to realize that projecting to the back of the house is your purpose. Balancing the craft and the art takes more than a year or two. Take every role offered and ply your craft until you can manage the many modes of acting being offered in the industry.

ARTICULATION

When you are on stage, you face an audience of 100 to 2,000 and your job is to project so that the person in the last row can enjoy the play. Projection is magical. Without an increase in volume **intend** to reach the person at the back of the theater audience – speak distinctly and enunciate the consonants. You should be understood without the help of a microphone.

Large theaters are miked across the front of the stage but projecting your part includes so much more than being heard.

There is something referred to as Stage English. Standardized pronunciation of vowels. Elocution. It's during this study that you may correct regionalisms, a sibilance or perfect dialects. A good British accent may come in handy during an acting career. And for Shakespeare one must speak the King's English.

Exercises designed to loosen your lips and tone your tongue:

Italian William, Italian William, Italian William, Italian William
Butta gutta butta gutta butta gutta butta gutta butta gutta
Gutta butta gutta butta gutta butta gutta butta gutta butta

On a musical triad – do-me-sol
Up and down the triad may may may may may
Same three notes ray ray ray ray ray
Then move up one note and repeat may then ray
All the way up the scale

This opens up the music in your voice passing notes that allow for subtlety in your expression.

If you have chosen a mumble as a psychological component of your character, it is incumbent upon you to project those mumbles to the person in the last row. This takes some doing. Without losing the fine touch of the mumble, focus that utterance so that it reaches the last row as a mumble. This is possible. It is intention at work here.

Projection is a tricky concept to master. Start with a Shakespearean sonnet.

> *"When in disgrace of fortune and men's eyes*
> *I all alone beweep my outcast state*
> *And trouble deaf heaven with my bootless cries"*

Project it across the street but without raising your voice, no shouting allowed. The best exercise of projection that I ran across came from a choreographer.

I was in my second year at the Playhouse and won a solo in the spring musical revue. The song was titled *I'm the Girl Who Sings in Front of the Curtain While They're Changing the Set Behind*. During the staging of the song Bob Haddad, a New York import, asked me to try an exercise. He took a cigarette out of a pack and handed it to me. He said, "sing the song to the cigarette."

Now I had been asked to play one of Cinderella's ugly step-sisters as a pig. I was used to goofy exercises. Being game I took it from the top. Lo and behold I found a new level of projection I'd never reached before. Focusing the song at one point gave the song to the audience.

MOTOR SKILLS

Another component of your acting chops is motor skills – ballet, yoga, jazz, fencing, judo, martial arts of every variety – all disciplines that develop flexibility, enhance your good looks, all that you call on to act – grief, fear, power, ecstasy, anger, exhilaration any and all emotions you might be called upon to act are expressed through body language. Remembering that it must be on a level that will project to the person in the last row. So any exercises to perfect those muscles of the body are measured as acting chops.

The stage itself is a place you need to find comfort on, mastery of, be at home on. Stand center stage. That would be half the distance from the front to the back and half the distance from the right side referred to as stage right and the left side referred to as stage left.

Up right, indicates the right side back and down left is the left side close to the front of the stage. By the way stage right is the actor's right not the audience' right.

Back in the days of vaudeville the front of the stage was called the **apron**. You may hear this nomenclature in the musical theater. That's where the chorus lines up.

Get used to making an entrance with your body remaining open. If you are entering down stage right you want to clear the stage opening using your left (upstage) foot. This is a better presentation than if you were to hit the stage on your right foot closing up your body and looking awkward. Exceptions can be made to customize an entrance but it lacks grace and calls attention to itself taking away from the play.

After playing little theaters and community theaters and make-shift theaters you finally arrive at a legitimate theater. Curtains and

everything. The big front curtain goes up to reveal the world of the play and closes to indicate the end of the play. The stage opening itself is called the **proscenium**. The curtain that hangs horizontally across the top masking the area that contains the drops is called a **teaser**. That space that contains the light fixtures and backdrops is called the **flies**. Those curtains that hang at the sides of the stage openings, stage right and stage left are referred to as **tormentors**. The immediate off stage areas are **wings**.

The director gives the cast the blocking for the play, you have the opportunity to perfect your stage movements. The director says enter downstage right and cross upstage left. Enter keeping your body open.

In all cases whether sitting, standing or moving keep the body open. When sitting, for example, cross the upstage leg over the downstage. It creates a much more attractive line than presenting the butt end of your downstage leg.

Stage turns. Avoid showing the audience your back. Unless of course it is for effect. But a good rule o' thumb is to arrange your turns allowing maximum exposure. For example, if you are in conversation with another center stage and are then exiting, set off on the upstage foot naturally opening your body before setting off.

Practice using props. Make a telephone call, pour a cup of tea, handle a hot potato, handle a gun. In any case involving a prop you want to be deliberate. Not mannered. But clean and precise. Handling props, referred to as **stage business** gives the actor another opportunity to sculpt something of the character's inner life.

The externals of acting are foundational and should never be overlooked. Comfort on stage is a great basis for building a character and it transmits to the audience quicker than any other skill that is required of an actor. When the actor is comfortable, the audience is given the license to get comfortable with him.

Relaxation is the key to prat-falls. The grace and relaxation required to pull off a stage fall are qualities that fencing and yoga practices will aid you with. During the practice of yoga, holding a pose permits consciousness other than your usual consciousness. This is not unlike inhabiting the body of your character.

It's customary to honor the pre-performance ritual of half hour. Thirty minutes before the scheduled curtain time the stage manager calls **Half hour** into his squawk box. You now have thirty minutes to apply make-up, dress and prepare to go onstage. During the time it is customary for actors to warm up their voices and/or do some physical exercise.

A theater company may take this preparation seriously. It's not unlikely that the entire company is invited to participate in such a ritual. An oft employed procedure known as **The Drop Down** begins with a centering of one's body with an even breathing cadence. Once centered you begin this drop-down by dropping your head to your chest. With your chin resting on your sternum continue to visualize each individual vertebra lift up and move upward floating over your body. Meanwhile your body continues to bend forward with each release of a vertebra. Your chest is now hanging from your spine. Continue to release your vertebra one at a time all the way to the bottom of your spine. You are now bent from the waist, your arms are hanging dead weight in front of you. Release your knees and voice an "ah". Let it fill your head cavity and moving up and down the scale warm up your vocal chords.

Shake out your head. Then prepare to reassemble your body. Slowly straighten your knees and stack each vertebra back in place. Keep working up the spine and when you get to the point of restoring your head, visualize a straight line that leaves your chin where it was meant to ride. Imagine you hang from a string puppet-like and notice that your chin doesn't jut out in this scenario. Relaxed, the chin doesn't dominate as is our habit as people who lead with their chin. This posture presents best onstage. The DropDown technique is derived from the Alexander Technique that I recommend you study. Google Alexander Technique to learn more.

So many adventures await you in New York. Though a job is hard to get and it is often short-lived, the constant shuffle becomes comfortable and when you survive the life so varied and colorful its fun!

I was in an off-broadway musical with Jerry Dodge. He was the original Barnaby in *Hello Dolly* and by the time I met him he was

moving on from Barnaby and seeking new adventure. We hit it off at the audition. We walked ten blocks before we parted. We both got the part! Opposite this popular, dashing, dance man with a glint in his eye and strut in his step, he was the personification of a star, made of star-dust no doubt.

We rehearsed in a theater in Paramus, New Jersey home of one of our producers, Robert Ludlum. The best-selling author had yet begun to write but he stood in the back of the theater in his trench coat not missing a beat. Jerry and I had a duet. "Gather Ye Rosebuds While Ye May" and the staging of the number was nothing swell. Jerry pulled me aside and said, "this number should be a showstopper, no?" "That would be grand", said I. "Let's restage it!" "What?" This had not been done in my experience. P.S. we did the new staging that night in the performance and it didn't stop the show. But the next day when I ran into Bob he threw a disapproving look and asked that I send Jerry to him when I ran into him. Jerry wasn't a diva but he did have a lot of George M. Cohan in him. No one forced us to go back to the original staging but we were nonetheless deflated. The show closed in a week.

The next summer, Jerry got a job at Stratford, the Shakespeare repertory company and Whit and I, Whitney Blausen was the costume designer for *Shoemaker's Holiday*, planned an adventure to see Jerry as Puck in *Midsummer's Night Dream*. Whit knew her way around and before I knew it we were headed for Stratford Connecticut and Gish Gables which was a house that actor's rented for the summer. It really was owned by the Gish sisters, Lillian and Dorothy, the silent movie stars. The house was a big old seaside home with a Captain's Walk, a small aisleway that ran across the second story that faced the sea.

AUDITION

The audition – **cold reading**. Grocery list – my rule o' thumb is to read the lines on the page as casually as possible. Honesty is what they are looking for. If you can deliver the lines with directness sans bad acting and you physically fit the character description, you are in.

Now for some acting approaches to avoid - there is a term for acting with no basis, it's **indication**. You are indicating that an emotion is being felt but you are not feeling it. Not good. So instead of giving a ham performance right off, choose to read the scene for sense.

You are usually given the **side**, another technical term. The 'side' is a copy of he scene alone without the rest of the script.

Look it over, break it into beats so that you have a map of the sense of the scene then deliver it dispassionately. If, as you play the scene, you awaken appropriate emotions, allow them in. Don't edit yourself at this stage. Should you earn a **call-back**, try to be yourself. Nerves and ambition take over and it may seem like coals to Newcastle but be yourself. Dress like the character.

Words of wisdom:

If you are a tomato and they're looking for a potato, you're not going to get the part.

Marlo Thomas's dad

Every kick is a boost.

Rue McClanahan's mom

EMOTIONAL MEMORY RECALL

To portray emotions, it's first necessary to become a fly on the wall.

Observe, observe, observe.

Get used to observing your own behavior first. As you express anger, love, piety, rage – watch yourself. Takes some getting used to. Get over the self-consciousness for this is very useful. Mastery of this skill takes a little time and then it's yours forever.

When you are acting, don't settle for stereotypical expression like hands on your hips to portray anger or indignation. That's indication. To show anger, take the time to do an emotional memory recall.

Reliving a strong emotive moment in your life will inform that moment in the play. But this time you live the anger. You are watching yourself so that you can use gestures, tensions, tones and feelings that arise and are genuine coming from your core.

Reliving the moment in your history that reflects the emotion you want to play begins by rebuilding the circumstances. Start by defining the room you were in where this moment occurred. Locate the light source. Try to recapture the smell, the air, feel your feet on the ground. Recall dialogue. What was said that ignited the greatest surge of emotion?

That memory will make that moment more accessible to you when it comes in the play. Now we are building the character from the inside.

The best lesson in emotional memory for me came in an exhibition by Brother Theodore during rehearsal for *Brigadoon*. Brother studied acting and directing at Catholic University and the world was cheated out of a great actor when he entered the Christian Brotherhood. I was in high school when I had the privilege of meeting and being directed

by Theodore Piperno. I went to acting school directly because of his influence.

We were a group of high schoolers who brought everything they had whether singing in the chorus, dancing in the ensemble or acting out the plot. I'd been in three prior productions directed by Brother and was acquainted with his penchant for heavy drama like when in exasperation he'd cancel the whole works. He had a flair.

This day Brother decided to play the part of Angus McClaren at the funeral of his son Charlie. From the moment Brother stepped onstage he embodied the emotion of the bereaved father. Not in any overwrought way but in the deep despair of losing a child and like a spreading fire everyone present wept in spite of ourselves. We all loved Charlie Jessup the actor who played Charlie and there wasn't a false note in this procession of mourners. The entire cast lived the burial scene together.

You won't have the luxury of a director arranging such a grand ensemble emotional memory but you will have the chance to create your own emotional memories befitting the role and the play in which you appear. Once you bring yourself to the height of the emotion, it will revive onstage when you re-enact it. Not that you produce fresh tears every time you reach that beat but the audience will be moved by the memory.

PERSONALIZATION

Another rarely discussed often overlooked skill is **personalization.** Go through the script and personalize any item that your character refers to or uses. Any item, memory or relationship that appears in the telling of the story needs to be personalized. This tool causes your acting to come alive like no other.

For instance, if your character is telling someone about a conversation they had, it is necessary to recreate that moment in your imagination so that when you recall it, it has the ring of truth. You aren't just speaking words, you recall that meeting.

This is true of relationships. If you speak of your grandma give her meat and bones, know what she looks like and sounds like. Know how you feel about her, how she feels about you.

There is so much work to be done at home as you work on a part. The more you can flesh out the details, the more reality you bring to the part. That is the sum total of a role. We are pieces on the chessboard acting out the motives and desires of mankind.

To subliminally communicate the character's inner life, it's useful to assign a psychological tic. An indecisive character may shrug his shoulders often, a would-be ballerina may point her toes. You must be judicious in the use of tics as they have been known to steal scenes.

Amateur actors always ask "what do I do with my arms?" Now if you have done the morning exercise of embodying your character, you know who you are on stage and whether you are delivering a line or not, you are engaged. If you aren't talking you need to be listening or involved in an onstage activity.

TALKING & LISTENING

Most critical if you remember nothing else remember **do not anticipate**. You are in the world of the play. Though you know the outcome you need to dial back all that and walk into a scene with a clean slate. You don't know what is going to happen.

Play your motivation hard and allow for surprises. Don't play "innocence" or "surprise"; that would be mugging and bad acting. But as you work on the scene in your mind, realize the deepening of understanding in both your character and the situation.

You never have to memorize your lines when you work through each scene mentally. Once you know why you are playing the scene you will find you know your lines.

A visual – imagine a thread attached to your words as you talk. Wait for a response. And then visualize that same thread coming back to you as you get a response. Now don't play "listening". That would be indication, mugging, bad acting in a big way. Sometimes I found myself using silent mental comments like "what did he just say?" When you are on camera especially it's advisable to have fully fleshed out mental thoughts .

The tempo of the scene will establish itself based on the give and take, back and forth, and most scenes of conflict escalate. Some may even crescendo. You may find that your character lacks an answer at some point. Then take what's called a pregnant pause. Think on the spot, go through the logical progression of thoughts that will give rise to your next attack, parry, pirouette – all terms I use in describing the mental gymnastics your character may use.

May I recommend the movie *The Best Years of Our Lives* and call your attention to the reactions the actors avail themselves of at the

end of final beats in a scene. This is obviously directed in by William Wyler and so effectively as to win him an Oscar. But this technique would add credibility and reality to your work as an actor.

People, while criticizing an acting job, remark on the **choices** an actor made. These choices spring from the inner life of the character. How that person expresses himself at peak moments of emotion tell us more than the dialogue is able.

It's what made Jimmy Dean's performance in *East of Eden* so memorable. His instinct for acting was very keen as we were to see in his varied and interesting characters. As Marlon Brando entertained us with his choices and characters; fleshing out a character is all the fun of acting.

Remembering is the last of the trio of subconscious realms that we access in acting and it comes up very often. Tennessee Williams uses this mode often; in fact, his one act *Talk to me Like the Rain and Let me Listen* is 99% remembering; the leading lady talks about her past. The most remarkable scene in *Master Class* is Maria Callas remembering her life with her abusive husband. Emotional memory recall is what ignites each of these cases.

Repeating and repeating the scream of terror that the lizard may jump in her direction, the girl in the commercial chose three notes do-re-mi and it remained her job to fill the outer shell every time with true emotion. The discussion this generates is one of method acting versus technical acting – Marlon Brando vs Laurence Olivier.

Neither can be discounted really. Marlon would totally deny that his STELLLLAAAA was anything less than a method scream, nightly, while he performed it on Broadway and repeatedly while he filmed it in Hollywood. But observing him, we undoubtedly heard the same note pitched every time he hollered her name. Though if you are "caught" just technically hitting the right notes without the underlying truth of the emotion you are said to be **phoning it in**. No no.

When you act as though you are acting, a bold black line forms cartoon-like around you as an outline. You don't want to be caught in this mode of bad acting either; this means you are acting not being.

COMMENTS

The best moment of acting I ever witnessed was Albert Finney in Act I scene 1 of John Osborne's play *Luther* on Broadway. Finney took a seizure on stage so realistically that I turned to my companion and said, "that's that. We're going home".

This week, some fifty years later, I watched an acting moment on cable television *Breaking Bad* where a young man lost a joint of a very lethal drug – out of his pocket? He dropped it? He had no idea how he'd lost it. He and his friend are sitting on the couch taking a pause from their search of the room when a Rumba moves across the screen. "What's that?" asks the friend. Cut to the opening up of the compartment where debris is sucked into the machine and lo and behold the joint is there.

Now we watch the young man's thought process, a mixture of relief and disbelief. Most amazingly, we watch his face <u>flush with color</u>! Then he turns and tears rushing down his cheeks admits that he almost shot his friend for having stolen this treasure. This entire moment was captured in one shot. The camera never moved. That one can act a flushed face proves how deep one can go in the depths of acting.

Working in summer stock I met a New York actor I admired. We discussed my plan to go to New York eventually and he counseled me that it takes one hundred auditions before you land a role. "Not for me", I thought. I lived to rue the day. It takes a while to learn the skill of auditioning and no amount of advice can replace the experience.

There is a newspaper called **BackStage** and in it is listed every audition being held for the coming week. Without representation, you are able to show up and audition. These parts are chorus but that is

a great place to start. Getting an agent appears to be an act of God. Once you do make that connection your odds go up. And you get face to face meetings with directors looking for a specific type.

Creating the world-of-the-play is adding cream to your porridge. This component of the art is so often overlooked. Personally I can tell when an actor has done his homework and when he hasn't.

Wait wait. I forgot a really good exercise. Looking over all these exercises I didn't include **as if.** When working on improvisations the director may say "all right everybody you have a half hour to live". He wants everyone to adopt that circumstance. It's simply known as an "as if". "As if" you've just been paralyzed, "As if" you've just lost your last dime, "As if" you've just won an Oscar. You get the idea.

As a youngster, I loved to sing. My mother entered me in a talent show being held in a movie theater. The big-time! Rehearsing at home I was ready to do a performance for mom. My song was *I'm Sitting on Top of the World.* When I finished she said, "I didn't believe you." Ouch! Back to the drawingboard. And the lesson lasted my entire career. There was her voice always beckoning truth, for heaven's sake.

PLAY LIST

Hedda Gabler	Henrik Ibsen
A Streetcar Named Desire	Tennessee Williams
The Cherry Orchard	Anton Chekhov
A Man For All Seasons	Robert Bolt
Who's Afraid of Virginia Woolf	Edward Albee
Skin of Our Teeth	Thornton Wilder
Oklahoma	Lynn Riggs
	– original Green Grow the Lilacs
Our Betters	Somerset Maugham
Angels in America	Tony Kushner
Master Class	Terrence McNally
Glengarry Glen Ross	David Mamet
Misalliance	George Bernard Shaw

Spanning centuries these plays are written to reflect not only the style of the period but the psychology of the times in which they were penned. To understand how we have developed there is no history more telling than that of theater literature.

AFTERWORD

When I arrived at the American Conservatory Theater, A.C.T., Bill Ball who was Founder of the company and its Director at the time stunned us all with his practices. His desire for his company to reach heights unknown for an acting company was expressed in his welcome packet distributed to everyone the first day of our meeting.

The mirrors in the rehearsal studio would be papered over. It was customary to have rehearsals mirrored for actors to consider the lines of their bodies. To work without mirrors was a shocking reminder that vanity was not welcome. And that the fourth wall, the imaginary wall in which the play is performed separating actors from audience was to be honored – in no way broken. Bill Ball was creating a circle of concentration. He went on to request that no one discuss a performance neither with criticism nor praise. We were invited to use the meditation room, meditating being a prerequisite of signing a contract.

Since the institute was a conservatory, there was no end of classes. Yoga, Alexander Technique, a voice coach guru who taught us all exercises to retain the youth in our voice.

Inspiration is contagious – connecting with a song, carried away by a piano concerto. In the repertory company the director once said "when you enter" he was addressing actors at curtain, "and find an actor on stage who is 'on fire' - hold your torch to that light and catch fire too."

ACKNOWLEDGEMENTS

Jean Knaiz
Brother Theodore Piperno
Konstantin Stanislavski
Ed Martz
Edith Skinner
Joe Layton
Bill Ball
Jerry Dodge
Bill Gerber
Milton Katselas
Paul Sills
Duncan Noble
Bob Haddad
Tommy Leonetti
Mary Alice Lewis
Whitney Blausen
Dick Lescsak

ABOUT THE AUTHOR

Daughter of an Austrian/Ukrainian father, Eugene, and a singularly Polish mother, Regina, Judah was raised on musical comedy and musical movies and a highly theatrical Catholic Church of the Franciscan Order with Gregorian Chant and Tennebrae.

Eugene was orphaned at sixteen months and Regina's parents spoke only Polish. Eugene taught Judah that telling a lie threw her life off course, off the path that God intended her to follow. Judah's mother was a talented singer and actress who passed her talents to her daughter.

Judah studied acting at the Pittsburgh Playhouse School of the Theater and was invited after graduating to join the acting staff of the Playhouse for two years. She did summer stock in the area's four local summer stock theaters.

New York, New York her first job was in a satiric revue at the Upstairs at the Downstairs and over the next seven years worked Off-Broadway and On Broadway and toured the country twice in National Tours. She was cast in a major motion picture. And landed a two year turn at ACT, the repertory theater in San Francisco.

Over the span of twenty years I learned so much from so many great talents and it seemed only appropriate to share what I had gathered. I highly recommend a life in the theater, though it isn't stable it is exhilarating to live as an artist.

www.ingramcontent.com/pod-product-compliance
Lightning Source LLC
Chambersburg PA
CBHW021923170526
45157CB00005B/2166